Design: Judith Chant and Alison Lee
Recipe Photography: Peter Barry
Jacket and Illustration Artwork: Jane Winton, courtesy of
Bernard Thornton Artists, London
Editors: Jillian Stewart and Kate Cranshaw

The publishers would like to thank Elaine Messenger at the
British Diabetic Association for her help with this book.

CLB 4258
Published by Grange Books, an imprint of Grange Books PLC,
The Grange, Grange Yard, London, SE1 3AG
© 1995 CLB Publishing, Godalming, Surrey, England.
All rights reserved
Printed and bound in Singapore
Published 1995
ISBN 1-85627-558-2

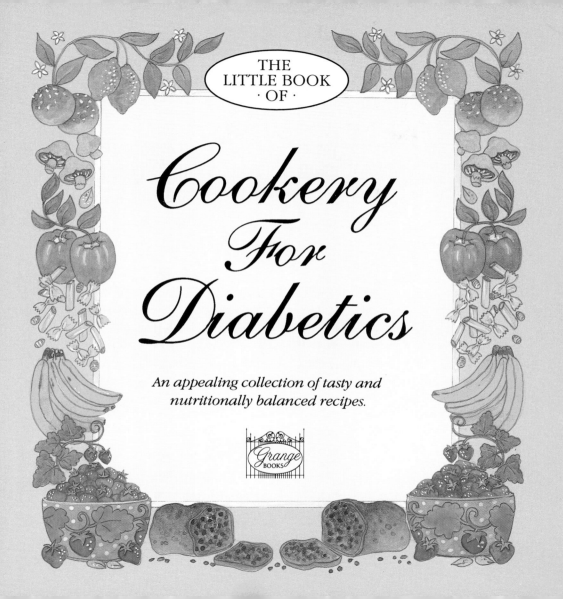

THE LITTLE BOOK · OF ·

Cookery For Diabetics

*An appealing collection of tasty and
nutritionally balanced recipes.*

Grange BOOKS

Introduction

Eating the right foods is crucial to the health of all diabetics and a well planned approach to recipe planning is one of the keys to making delicious, well-balanced menus part of your everyday life.

This book is not intended as a guide book for diabetics, but simply as an extra source of carbohydrate and calorie counted recipes for diabetics who already know their dietary requirements and can confidently incorporate these recipes into their diet plan. There is no substitute for the the tailor-made advice which every diabetic should receive from a qualified dietician when they are diagnosed.

Although individuals should be aware of their specific needs, there are a number of general guidelines which apply to the diabetic diet. Eating too much food at any one time should be avoided as it results in too much glucose for the system to cope with adequately. It is therefore advisable to have smallish meals and a variety of snacks throughout the day. This is particularly relevant to diabetics taking insulin, who should coincide their meals with the availability of insulin. Also important is the type of meal eaten. Those foods which are digested slowly further help to 'spread' the release of glucose into the blood. Carbohydrate foods that contain a significant amount of dietary fibre or roughage are particularly important for this purpose as not only do they take longer to digest, but a high fibre diet helps to lower blood sugar levels. Finally, fat is another factor particularly relevant to diabetics. As diabetics are recommended to eat fibre-rich carbohydrate, a corresponding reduction in fat intake is often necessary if excess weight gain is to be avoided. Excess fat intake is also recognised as a major contributor to heart disease, and diabetics are already at a disadvantage as diabetes is recognised as a risk factor in developing such conditions.

The advice given to diabetics to follow a high-fibre, low-fat diet is advice that most people, diabetic or not, would be well advised to follow, and obviously as this pattern of eating becomes more commonplace so the range and availability of suitable ingredients increases. Hopefully, you will find some inspiring recipes in this little cookbook, and eventually gain the confidence to create your own. Obviously you will have to be very aware of your own particular dietary requirements but the following tips may also be of some help:

- When using artificial sweeteners ensure they are completely sugar-free
- Use wholemeal flour wherever possible
- Use wholemeal pasta and brown rice in place of their more refined cousins
- Fortify appropriate dishes such as soups and stews with pulses as they add valuable fibre
- Low-fat or reduced-fat cheeses should be used in place of full-fat cheeses
- Polyunsaturated oils such as sunflower, and polyunsaturated and mono-unsaturated margarines should be used
- All visible fat should be trimmed from chicken and meat
- Use low-fat yogurt in place of cream wherever possible

Celery and Apple Soup

SERVES 4

This unusual combination of ingredients produces a tasty soup which is ideal as a starter or lunch dish when served with crusty wholemeal rolls.

PREPARATION: 15 mins
COOKING: 45 mins
TOTAL CARBOHYDRATE: 60g PER SERVING: 15g
TOTAL ENERGY: 468 kcals PER SERVING: 117 kcals

30g/1oz polyunsaturated margarine
1 large onion, finely chopped
3 cooking apples, cored and sliced
1.2 litres/2 pints vegetable stock
1 bay leaf
Salt and freshly ground black pepper
3 sticks celery, finely chopped
Finely sliced celery, to garnish

1. Melt the margarine in a large pan and stir in the onion. Fry gently for 5 minutes, or until the onion is soft but not browned.

2. Add the apple to the onion mixture and cook for a further 3 minutes, or until the apple begins to soften.

3. Stir half the stock into the onion and apple, along with the bay leaf and seasoning. Bring to the boil, cover and simmer for 30 minutes. Remove the bay leaf.

4. Put the remaining stock into another pan along with the celery. Bring to the boil, then cover and simmer for 30 minutes.

5. Using a liquidiser or food processor, blend the onion and apple mixture until smooth.

6. Whisk the puréed onion and apple mixture into the pan containing the stock and celery.

7. Return the pan to the heat and bring back to the boil. Serve immediately and garnish with the finely sliced celery.

Salmon Paté

SERVES 4

This highly nutritious, elegant paté is low in fat and very quick to prepare. Serve as a starter with a salad garnish, and accompany with melba toast or brown bread.

PREPARATION: 15 mins, plus chilling
TOTAL CARBOHYDRATE: 10g PER SERVING:
    negligible
TOTAL ENERGY: 669 kcals PER SERVING: 167 kcals

225g/8oz canned red or pink salmon, drained
150g/5oz low fat curd cheese
Few drops of lemon juice
Pinch of ground mace or nutmeg
¼ tsp Tabasco sauce
Salt and freshly ground black pepper
2 tbsps 1% fat fromage frais, or low fat natural
    yogurt
4 small gherkins

---

1. Remove the bones and skin from the salmon. Place the fish in the bowl of a food processor and work briefly to break it up.

2. Add the curd cheese and work the machine in bursts until the mixture is smooth and well combined.

3. Add the lemon juice, seasonings and fromage frais and process briefly until all the ingredients are well mixed.

4. Divide the mixture between 4 individual ramekins and smooth the surfaces. Chill before serving.

5. Slit each gherkin lengthways 4 or 5 times, making sure that you do not cut completely through the narrow end. Fan the gherkins out and use these to garnish the top of the paté.

Step 5 Slice each gherkin lengthways, 4 or 5 times, taking care not to cut right through the narrow end. Spread out into fan shapes.

Pork with Green Peppers

SERVES 4

This quickly prepared stir-fried dish is ideal for a quick lunch or supper dish. Serve with brown rice or noodles.

PREPARATION: 15 mins
COOKING: 6 mins
TOTAL CARBOHYDRATE: 10g PER SERVING:
   negligible
TOTAL ENERGY: 930 kcals PER SERVING:
   233 kcals

460g/1lb pork fillet
2 tbsps sunflower oil
1 clove garlic, crushed
2 green peppers, cut into thin strips
1 tsp wine vinegar
2 tbsps chicken stock
1 tbsp Hoisin sauce
Salt and pepper
1 tsp cornflour, mixed with a little water

1. Slice the pork thinly, then cut into narrow strips.

Step 1 Slice the pork thinly, then cut into narrow strips.

2. Heat the oil in a wok, add the garlic, green pepper, and the meat. Mix together well and stir-fry for 1 minute.

3. Stir in the vinegar, stock and Hoisin sauce. Season to taste and cook for a further 3 minutes.

4. Stir in the cornflour mixture and cook, stirring constantly, until the sauce is thickened.

Chicken Stuffed Peppers

SERVES 6

Using chicken as a stuffing for peppers makes a lighter dish than the more usual meat stuffing. Serve either hot or cold and accompany with rice and salad for a lunch or supper dish.

PREPARATION: 30 mins
COOKING: 45-50 mins
TOTAL CARBOHYDRATE: 160g PER SERVING: 30g
TOTAL ENERGY: 2704 kcals PER SERVING:
    450 kcals

3 large green or red peppers
30g/1oz polyunsaturated margarine
1 small onion, finely chopped
1 stick celery, finely chopped
1 clove garlic, crushed
3 chicken breasts, skinned, boned and diced
2 tsps chopped parsley
Salt and freshly ground black pepper
½ loaf stale wholemeal bread, made into
    crumbs
1-2 eggs, beaten
6 tsps dry brown breadcrumbs

Step 1 Cut the peppers in half and remove the cores and seeds.

1. Cut the peppers in half lengthways and remove the cores and seeds. Leave the stems attached, if wished.

2. Melt the margarine in a frying pan and add the onion, celery, garlic and chicken. Cook over a moderate heat until the vegetables are softened and the chicken is cooked. Add the parsley and season with salt and pepper.

3. Stir in the stale breadcrumbs and add enough beaten egg to make the mixture hold together.

4. Spoon the filling into each pepper half, mounding the top slightly. Place the peppers in a baking dish that holds them closely together.

5. Pour enough water around the peppers to come about 1.25cm/½-inch up their sides. Cover and bake in an oven preheated to 180°C/350°F/Gas Mark 4, for about 45 minutes or until the peppers are just tender.

6. Sprinkle each pepper with the dried crumbs and place under a preheated grill until golden brown.

Fisherman's Stew

SERVES 6

This quick, economical and satisfying dish will please any fish fan. It makes an ideal meal for lunch or supper if served with brown rice, salad, or extra French bread.

PREPARATION: 20 mins
COOKING: 45 mins
TOTAL CARBOHYDRATE: 100g PER SERVING: 25g
TOTAL ENERGY: 2413 kcals PER SERVING:
   403 kcals

60ml/4 tbsps olive oil
2 large onions, sliced
1 red pepper, sliced
120g/4oz mushrooms, sliced
460g/1lb canned tomatoes
Sprig dried thyme
Salt and freshly ground black pepper, to taste
420ml/¾ pint water
900g/2lbs firm, white fish fillets, skinned and
   cut into chunks
140ml/¼ pint white wine or fish stock and
   wine mixed
2 tbsps chopped parsley
120g/4oz French stick, sliced and toasted

---

1. Heat the oil in a large saucepan and add the onions and cook until beginning to look

Step 1 Add the red pepper to the onions and cook until softened.

translucent. Add the red pepper and cook until softened.

2. Add the mushrooms and the tomatoes and bring the mixture to the boil.

3. Add the thyme, seasoning and water, and simmer for 30 minutes

4. Add the fish and wine and cook for 10-15 minutes or until the fish is opaque and starts to flake. Carefully stir in the parsley.

5. To serve, place a piece of French bread in the bottom of each of 6 soup plates and carefully spoon the stew over.

Savoury Bean Pot

SERVES 4

Use canned kidney beans or other canned beans to make this dish easy and quick to prepare. Serve with wholewheat pasta or brown rice.

PREPARATION: 20 mins
COOKING: 45 mins
TOTAL CARBOHYDRATE: 160g PER SERVING: 40g
TOTAL ENERGY: 1085 kcals PER SERVING:
   271 kcals

---

2 tbsps olive or sunflower oil
2 vegetable stock cubes, crumbled
2 medium onions
2 dessert apples, grated
2 carrots, grated
3 tbsps tomato purée
280ml/½ pint water
2 tbsps white wine vinegar
1 tbsp mustard powder
1 tsp dried oregano
1 tsp cumin
Artificial sweetener equivalent to 2 tsps sugar
Salt and freshly ground black pepper
460g/1lb cooked red kidney beans
2 tbsps low fat yogurt (optional)

1. Heat the oil in a non-stick pan. Add the crumbled stock cubes, onions, apples and carrots. Sauté for 5 minutes, stirring occasionally.

2. Mix the tomato purée with the water and add together with all the other ingredients apart from the beans and yogurt.

3. Stir the mixture well, cover and simmer for 2 minutes.

4. Add the beans to the pan and stir in well, then tip the mixture into an ovenproof casserole.

5. Bake, covered, in an oven preheated to 180°C/350°F/Gas Mark 4, for 35-40 minutes.

6. Look at the casserole after 20 minutes and add a little more water if necessary. To serve, top with swirls of low fat yogurt, if wished.

Sweet Pepper Steaks

SERVES 4

In this tasty dish, peppers, mustard and capers blend together to make a delicious spicy sauce for beef steak. Serve with either brown rice or jacket potatoes and broccoli.

PREPARATION: 30 mins, plus standing time
COOKING: 20 mins
TOTAL CARBOHYDRATE: 80g PER SERVING: 20g
TOTAL ENERGY: 1825 kcals PER SERVING:
   456 kcals

---

4 sirloin steaks, about 120g/4oz each
2 cloves garlic, crushed
Freshly ground black pepper
3 tbsps olive or sunflower oil
2 shallots, finely chopped
60ml/4 tbsps capers
120g/4oz mushrooms, sliced
2 tbsps plain flour
280ml/½ pint dark stock
4 tsps mustard
2 tsps Worcestershire sauce
120ml/8 tbsps white wine
2 tsps lemon juice
Pinch each dried thyme and rosemary
8 baby corn cobs, halved lengthways
1 green pepper, sliced
1 red pepper, finely sliced
1 yellow pepper, finely sliced
4 tomatoes, skinned, seeded and cut into
   thin strips

---

1. Place the steaks on a board and remove the excess fat. Rub both surfaces of each steak with

the garlic and black pepper. Refrigerate for 30 minutes.

2. Heat the oil in a large frying pan and quickly fry the steaks for 1 minute on each side. Remove the steaks from the pan and set aside.

3. Add the shallots, capers and mushrooms to the oil and meat juices in the frying pan. Cook for about 1 minute.

4. Sprinkle the flour over the vegetables and fry gently until it begins to brown. Pour in the stock, stirring constantly. Add the mustard, Worcestershire sauce, wine, lemon juice and herbs as the sauce thickens.

5. Return the steaks to the sauce mixture along with the baby corn cobs, peppers and tomatoes. Simmer for 6-8 minutes, or until the steaks are cooked, but still pink in the centre. Serve at once.

Step 5 Stir the sweetcorn, peppers and tomatoes into the sauce, mixing well to coat evenly.

Farfalle with Tomato Sauce

SERVES 4

This is a great favourite with pasta fans – simple, delicious, and it looks good too!

PREPARATION: 10 mins
COOKING: 30 mins
TOTAL CARBOHYDRATE: 180g PER SERVING: 45g
TOTAL ENERGY: 2141 kcals PER SERVING:
    310 kcals

---

1 tbsp olive oil
2 cloves garlic, crushed
1 onion, sliced
½ tsp dried basil
2 × 400g/14oz cans chopped plum tomatoes
Salt and freshly ground black pepper
275g/10oz farfalle (pasta bows)
2 tbsps chopped fresh basil

---

1. Heat the oil in a deep pan. Add the garlic and onion and cook until softened. Add the dried basil and cook for 30 seconds.

2. Add the undrained tomatoes and season well. Bring to the boil, reduce the heat and simmer, uncovered, for about 20 minutes, or until the sauce is reduced by half.

3. Meanwhile, cook the pasta in a large pan of boiling, salted water for about 10 minutes or

Step 3 Add the undrained tomatoes to the pan.

until 'al dente'. Rinse in hot water and drain well.

4. Push the sauce through a sieve, and stir in the fresh basil. Toss the sauce through the pasta and serve immediately.

Step 4 Push the sauce through a sieve.

Poulet au Limon

SERVES 4

Roast chicken with a tang of lime makes an elegant yet quickly-made entrée. Serve with salad and bread or new potatoes and some vegetables.

PREPARATION: 25 mins, plus 4 hours marinating
COOKING: 35 mins
TOTAL CARBOHYDRATE: 10g PER SERVING: negligible
TOTAL ENERGY: 1581 kcals PER SERVING: 395 kcals

2 × 900g/2lb chickens
1 tsp basil
2 tbsps olive oil
4 limes
Salt and freshly ground black pepper
Artificial sweetener, to taste (optional)

1. Remove the leg ends and wing tips from the chickens.

2. Split each chicken in half lengthways, cutting away the backbone completely and discarding it. Remove the skin.

3. Loosen the ball and socket joint in the leg and flatten each half of the chicken by hitting it with the flat side of a cleaver.

4. Season the chicken on both sides with salt and pepper and sprinkle over the basil. Place the chicken in a shallow dish and pour over the oil. Squeeze the juice from two of the limes and pour over the chicken. Cover and leave to

Step 3 Bend the chicken legs backwards to loosen the ball and socket joints.

marinate in the refrigerator for 4 hours or overnight.

5. Transfer the chicken to a roasting tin and sprinkle with some of the marinade. Place in an oven preheated to 190°C/375°F/Gas Mark 5, and roast for about 25 minutes, or until the juices run clear when pierced with a skewer. Baste the chicken occasionally with the marinade.

6. Cut off all the peel and pith from the remaining limes and slice them thinly. When the chicken is cooked, place the lime slices on top of the chicken and heat quickly under the grill. Add a little sweetener to the limes if wished.

7. Place the chicken in a serving dish and spoon over the cooking juices. Serve immediately.

Andalusian Aubergines

SERVES 4

Tomatoes, rice and tuna fish are very popular ingredients in Spain, and they make a delicious stuffing for aubergines. Serve with a mixed salad, black olives and bread.

PREPARATION: 40 mins
COOKING: 50 mins
TOTAL CARBOHYDRATE: 70g PER SERVING: 20g
TOTAL ENERGY: 754 kcals PER SERVING: 189 kcals

4 small aubergines
2 tbsps olive oil
1 small onion, finely chopped
1 clove garlic, crushed
120g/4oz cooked brown rice
200g/7oz can tuna in brine, drained and flaked
1 tbsp 1% fat fromage frais or low fat yogurt
1 tsp curry powder
4 tomatoes, skinned, seeded and chopped
1 tbsp coarsely chopped parsley
Salt and freshly ground black pepper

1. Cut the aubergines in half lengthways. Score the cut surfaces lightly with a sharp knife at regular intervals in a lattice pattern.

2. Brush the scored surfaces with 1 tbsp of the oil and place the aubergines on a greased baking sheet.

3. Bake the aubergines in an oven preheated to 190°C/375°F/Gas Mark 5, for 15 minutes or until beginning to soften.

Step 1 Taking care not to break the skins, score the cut surfaces of the aubergine halves at regular intervals.

4. Cool the aubergines slightly, then carefully scoop out the centre flesh from each half, taking care not to break the skins.

5. Sauté the onion gently in the remaining oil for 3 minutes or until transparent.

6. Add the garlic and the aubergine flesh and fry for a further 2 minutes.

7. Add the rice, tuna, fromage frais, curry powder, tomatoes, parsley and season to taste.

8. Mix the ingredients together well then spoon equal amounts into the aubergine shells. Brush the aubergines with a little oil, return them to the oven on the baking sheet and bake for a further 25 minutes.

Leila's Salad

SERVES 4

This salad makes an ideal light lunch if served with crusty wholemeal bread.

PREPARATION: 15 mins
COOKING: 30-35 mins
TOTAL CARBOHYDRATE: 130g PER SERVING: 35g
TOTAL ENERGY: 958 kcals PER SERVING:
    240 kcals

275g/10oz long grain brown rice
225g/8oz pineapple, chopped
1 bunch spring onions, finely chopped
60g/2oz flaked almonds, lightly toasted
½ bunch radishes, finely sliced
90g/3oz bean sprouts
Twists of lime, to garnish

Dressing
3 tbsps sunflower oil
1 tbsp sherry
Juice of 1 lime
1 tsp grated root ginger
Salt and freshly ground black pepper, to taste

---

1. Cook the rice in boiling salted water for 30-35 minutes, or until tender. Drain and allow to cool.

2. Combine the rice with the pineapple, spring onions, almonds, radishes and bean sprouts. If using fresh bean sprouts, blanch them in boiling water for 2 minutes then refresh in cold water before using.

3. Mix all the dressing ingredients together in a bowl and whisk with a fork until well incorporated.

4. Pour the dressing over the salad and fold in carefully. Refrigerate until required then garnish with the lime twists.

Courgette Salad

SERVES 6

Raw vegetables are full of vitamins, and although courgette seems an unlikely vegetable to eat raw it has a delicious flavour and texture. Serve this salad as an accompaniment to cold meat or poultry.

PREPARATION: 15 mins, plus 30 mins chilling
COOKING: 10 mins
TOTAL CARBOHYDRATE: 60g PER SERVING: 10g
TOTAL ENERGY: 1056 kcals PER SERVING:
    176 kcals

225g/8oz wholewheat macaroni
4 tomatoes
4-5 courgettes, thinly sliced
8 stuffed green olives, sliced
90ml/6 tbsps fat-free French dressing

---

1. Put the macaroni in a large saucepan and cover with plenty of boiling water. Add some salt and cook for 10-12 minutes, or until 'al dente'. Rinse in cold water and drain well.

2. Cut a small cross in the tops of the tomatoes and plunge into boiling water for about 30 seconds.

3. Drain them and cover with cold water then remove the loosened skins, using a sharp knife. Remove the cores and seeds of the tomatoes and coarsely chop the flesh.

4. Mix all the ingredients in a large bowl and chill for 30 minutes before serving.

Step 1 Rinse the cooked macaroni in cold water, then drain well forking it to prevent it sticking together.

Step 4 Mix all the ingredients together well, stirring thoroughly to blend the dressing in evenly.

Flageolet Fiesta

SERVES 4

Serve this dish on its own as a starter or as a side dish. Red kidney beans can be used instead of the flageolet beans.

PREPARATION: 15 mins, plus 2 hours marinating
COOKING: 1 hour
TOTAL CARBOHYDRATE: 60g PER SERVING: 15g
TOTAL ENERGY: 865 kcals PER SERVING: 216 kcals

225g/8oz cooked flageolet beans
1 medium onion
1 clove garlic
½ cucumber
2 tbsps chopped parsley
2 tbsps chopped mint
2 tbsps olive oil
Juice and grated rind of 1 lemon
Salt and freshly ground black pepper
Watercress, to garnish

1. Put the cooked beans in a mixing bowl.

2. Peel and finely chop the onion.

3. Crush the garlic and chop the cucumber into bite-sized pieces.

4. Add the onion, garlic, cucumber, herbs, oil, lemon juice and rind to the beans and mix well.

5. Add seasoning to taste and leave to marinate for 2 hours.

6. Transfer to a clean serving dish and garnish with watercress before serving.

Strawberry Cloud

Tofu blended with strawberries makes a tasty, quick and healthy dessert that is ideal for summer. Other fruit such as apricots, peaches, mangoes or pitted cherries would taste equally delicious.

PREPARATION: 10 mins
TOTAL CARBOHYDRATE: 30g PER SERVING: 10g
TOTAL ENERGY: 372 kcals PER SERVING: 93 kcals

460g/1lb strawberries
1 × 275g/10oz pack silken tofu
Juice of ½ lemon
Artificial sweetener, to taste
Few drops vanilla essence

1. Wash and hull the strawberries, reserve a few for decoration then roughly chop the rest.

2. Drain the tofu and put into a liquidiser together with the strawberries and lemon juice. Liquidise until smooth.

3. Add the liquid sweetener and vanilla essence to taste, mixing in well.

4. Divide the mixture between 4-6 individual serving dishes and decorate with the reserved strawberries. Chill until required.

Almond-Stuffed Figs

SERVES 4
*Fresh figs are now easily available from most major supermarkets and good greengrocers,
but if unavailable fresh peach halves would work equally well.*

PREPARATION: 20 mins
TOTAL CARBOHYDRATE: 60g PER SERVING: 15g
TOTAL ENERGY: 560 kcals PER SERVING: 140 kcals

---

4 large ripe figs
45g/4 tbsps ground almonds
2 tbsps orange juice
2 tbsps finely chopped dried apricots
60ml/4 tbsps low fat natural yogurt
Finely grated rind of ½ orange
Wedges of fig and mint or strawberry leaves, to
    decorate

---

1. Cut each fig into quarters using a sharp knife, taking care not to cut right down through the base.

Step 2 Ease the four sections of each fig outwards to form a flower shape.

Step 4 Divide the almond mixture evenly between the four figs, and press it into the centre of each one.

2. Ease the four sections of each fig outwards to form a flower shape.

3. Put the ground almonds, orange juice and chopped apricots into a small bowl and mix together thoroughly.

4. Divide the mixture into four, and press it into the centre of each fig.

5. For the sauce, mix together the yogurt and orange rind, then thin it down slightly with a little water or more orange juice.

6. Spoon a small pool of orange yogurt onto each of four serving plates, and sit a stuffed fig in the centre of each pool. Decorate with the additional wedges of fig and the mint or strawberry leaves.

Baked Bananas Sauce à La Poire

SERVES 4

Baked bananas are an established favourite dessert and served with this delightful fruity sauce they are particularly delicious.

PREPARATION: 10 mins
COOKING: 10 mins
TOTAL CARBOHYDRATE: 100g PER SERVING: 25g
TOTAL ENERGY: 422 kcals PER SERVING: 105 kcals

2 small oranges
2 ripe pears, peeled and cored
Artificial sweetener, to taste
2 bananas

1. Using a potato peeler pare the rind from one of the oranges, taking care not to include too much white pith.

2. Cut the pared rind into very thin strips with a sharp knife and blanch in boiling water for 2-3 minutes, to soften. Drain and set aside.

3. Peel and segment one orange and squeeze the juice from the other.

4. Place the orange juice and pears in a food processor, purée until smooth. Sweeten to taste.

5. Peel the bananas and halve them lengthways. Place in an oven-proof dish and pour the pear purée over the top. Cover and bake in an oven preheated to 180°C/350°F/Gas Mark 4, for 10 minutes or until the bananas are soft.

6. Decorate with orange segments and strips of orange rind. Serve immediately.

Apple Spice Ring

SERVES 10
This delicious and healthy cake can be served hot as a dessert with apple purée.

PREPARATION: 15 mins
COOKING: 45 mins
TOTAL CARBOHYDRATE: 170g PER SERVING: 20g
TOTAL ENERGY: 1588 kcals PER SERVING:
    159 kcals

460g/1lb dessert apples, cored
90g/3oz ground hazelnuts
120g/4oz wholemeal flour
30g/1oz bran
1½ tsps baking powder
1 tsp ground cinnamon
Pinch of ground nutmeg
Pinch of ground cardamom
30g/1oz polyunsaturated margarine
120ml/8 tbsps skimmed milk
Dessert apple slices, to decorate

---

1. Grate the apples on the coarse side of a grater.

2. Place in a mixing bowl along with the hazelnuts.

3. Stir in the flour, bran, baking powder and spices. Mix to blend well.

4. Add the margarine and beat until it is evenly blended.

5. Stir in the milk and mix to a stiff batter.

6. Carefully spoon into a greased 20.5cm/8-inch ring tin and level the top.

7. Bake in an oven preheated to 180°C/350°F/Gas Mark 4, for 45 minutes or until a skewer inserted into the centre of the cake comes out clean.

8. Allow to cool in the tin slightly then transfer to a wire rack to cool.

9. Decorate with apple slices just before serving.

Fruit Loaf

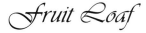

MAKES 2 loaves, each loaf makes 18 slices

Use any combination of your favourite dried fruits in this recipe for a variation. It is worth making two loaves as they will freeze for up to two months if wrapped in foil.

PREPARATION: about 2 hours
COOKING: 35-40 mins
TOTAL CARBOHYDRATE: 320g (per loaf) PER SLICE: 20g
TOTAL ENERGY: 1557 kcals (per loaf) PER SLICE: 87 kcals

460g/1lb strong wholemeal flour
½ tsp cinnamon
½ tsp nutmeg
½ tsp salt
225g/8oz sultanas
225g/8oz currants
60g/2oz cut mixed peel
1 sachet of easy-blend yeast
2 tbsps sunflower oil
About 280ml/½ pint lukewarm skimmed milk
1 large egg

---

1. Put the flour, spices and salt into a large mixing bowl. Stir in the dried fruit and peel, mixing well to distribute it evenly.

2. Sprinkle over the yeast, and mix this directly into the dry ingredients.

3. Put the oil, milk and egg into a large jug and beat together with a fork until the egg is broken up evenly. Add the mixture to the flour and mix together, stirring until the batter becomes soft and elastic.

4. Turn the dough onto a lightly floured board, and knead for about 10 minutes or until smooth.

5. Return the dough to the bowl and cover with a damp cloth or a piece of cling film. Leave to rise in a warm place for about 1 hour or until doubled in size.

6. Knock the dough back to remove the air, and turn it out onto the surface again. Knead the dough for about 5 minutes then cut it in two.

7. Shape each piece of dough to fit 2 × 18cm/7-inch non-stick loaf tins. Cover each loaf as before and leave in a warm place until doubled in size.

8. Bake in an oven preheated to 200°C/400°F/Gas Mark 6 for 35-40 minutes, removing them after 20 minutes to brush the tops with a little milk to glaze. The loaves are cooked when they sound hollow when tapped underneath.

Index

2/17